HOW TEACHERS POSITION BLACK BOYS IN ONTARIO'S K-12 SCHOOLS

CHARMAINE SIMMS-SAUNDERS
M.ED., B.ED.

DEDICATION

This book is dedicated to my late father, John George Simms, who died on December 10, 2019. Dad was proud of my accomplishments and his pride gave me strength to complete this book.

This book is also dedicated to my two sons, Daniel Saunders and Jordan Saunders, who were positioned by some of their K-12 teachers. They have repositioned themselves and are currently pursuing their undergraduate degree.

FORWARD

The treatment of Black boys in our modern school system is inspired by colonial times and slavery.

'Zero tolerance' policies had ensured that Black boys, based on societal prejudgment of their position in society, are to be punished more often than their student counterparts from other races.

In Ontario, Black boys are labelled by prejudgments of the educators who should be catering to their academic future. They are judged by educational policies that indicate that punishment or 'zero-tolerance' is no longer a rule, but this modernized update to school policies has not translated to the actual experience of the Black students.

This book presents a concept that is called Culturally Responsive Training – An opportunity for the Ontario educational system to implement a system that enables the school community to become more educated about the culture of the students that it is supposed to be serving.

CONTENTS

ABSTRACT

This book argues that to improve the academic success of Black boys in Ontario schools, educators need to better understand how they have been positioned in ways that have disadvantaged them academically. A discussion of positionality theory is provided and used as the basis for the development of a framework intended to assist teachers in developing culturally responsive teaching practices.

INTRODUCTION

The purpose of this book is to address the disproportionate experience of Black boys in Ontario schools when compared with their white counterparts in the same settings.

Referencing a 2017 study, over the years, Black boys have reported how they felt unwelcome in schools because they are monitored and corrected for minor infractions.

Furthermore, in the periodicals and files maintained by Ontario's Human Rights Commission, there are well-documented anti-Black allegations. These documents describe several stories of teachers in the school system and how they position Black boys in schools.

By depending on several research sources, the testimonials indicate that these children are marginalized as immigrants, fatherless, deviant, culturally deficient, not disciplined, hypermasculine, hyperphysical, hypersexual, disruptive, troublemakers, athletic, at-risk, and insubordinate.

These stereotypes have given rise to an educational issue that has influenced the development of this book.

To understand how teachers often classify Black boys in their teaching strata, it is useful to first understand the lasting effects of colonialism on educational culture in Canada.

Colonialism is the backdrop of this discourse. It is the reason why the disproportionate system in the education of Black boys exists. It is the albatross in the structure of our educational system which refuses to budge.

This book will provide background information on colonialism to give an understanding of how its legacy has influenced the way teachers position Black boys in Ontario's K-12 (kindergarten to grade 12) schools.

This gives way to an examination of 'positioning' theory and positionality, which are the premises on which this book is laid.

To summarize the purpose of this writing:

- The principal focus of this material will be varied. It will be an examination of the issue on how "Black boys" are positioned in ways that have served to undermine their educational experience

- The implications of the "Black" stereotype on these children's educational activities

- The continual application of zero tolerance when executing punishments

- The adoption of culturally responsive teaching

The data in this book will allow readers to assess how the removal of the words "zero tolerance" *from* the Ontario

Ministry's documents has not decreased the actual *occurrence* of an astoundingly high number of Black boys' detentions, suspensions, and expulsions. In other words, an absence of the practice from the books has not translated into action being taken regarding its removal from reality.

By examining positioning and its implications, this book provides an intervention to address this education issue through the adoption of a culturally responsive teaching (CRT) practice that is intended to help address the educational needs of Black boys.

Consequently, the positioning theory is used as the basis for the development of a conceptual PICRT (positioning, implications, and culturally responsive teaching) framework.

"Our true nationality
is mankind."
- H.G. Wells

CHAPTER ONE
COLONIALISM IN CANADA AND ITS LEGACY OF BLACK BOYS' POSITIONING

Anyone familiar with the history of Canada knows that the Indigenous people were its original inhabitants.

In the early 1500s, Canada was one of the countries colonized by the Europeans. Let us paint a picture of what this means: When a country or society is colonized, it would entail an invasion by settlers or aggressive 'conquerors' from another nation who sought to lay claim to that society as theirs to control.

When a society falls to the rulership of another nation's control, that society has effectively been colonized. Canada's colonialization story began as early as January 15, 1540 through the appointment of Jean-François de la Rocque de Sieur Roberval. Jean-François was a French nobleman and adventurer. France sent him to the settlement for the purpose of forming a colony out of Canada, Newfoundland, and Labrador, the settlements that existed on the land at the time.

You may ask the question – Why would France – or any other nation at the time – engage in colonization? What was the benefit of it?

One of the purposes of colonization is economic gains. The colonists seek to acquire new territories to expand the ability and opportunity of enrichment for their royal and upper-class society members in their own countries.

Therefore, in the early 1600s, in addition to conquering the land and taking charge of its resources, the French colonists required labour to harvest or mine those resources for the afore-mentioned economic gain that they were seeking.

Clearly, using labour from their own lands would require payment of wages. Therefore, a cheap way to accomplish the ends of labour shortages, and to reap economic benefits off the land at the cheapest cost possible, was to employ the use of *labour that cost nothing.*

This led to the beginning of slave trade in Canada: Blacks that were captured and shipped from their countries in Africa were, clearly, and as history depicts, not paid for their labour efforts. They were the answer to the labour shortage issue that was plaguing the colonized territories such as Canada.

Global trade of Black slaves from Africa had already begun by the 1600s. These helpless individuals were brought to Canada as labourers and were subjected to dehumanization.

This is probably a good place to talk about the story of Marie-Joseph Angélique, and to paint a picture of how little the colonists valued the lives of the slaves that they had captured from their homelands.

Marie-Joseph Angélique

Marie-Joseph was a black slave in Quebec in the 17th century. She was the slave of Francoise Francheville of Montreal. In 1734, a fire erupted on the land housing a group of properties belonging to her master, burning about 46 buildings on

Francheville's property. The rumour that spread about this incident was that the slave, Marie-Joseph had set the property on fire in order to escape to New England with her white lover. She was captured and based on the circumstantial evidence of twenty witnesses, she was hanged on June 21, 1734.

It was a baseless disregard for human life but was considered appropriate, according to the social and moral values of the colonial times.

Power and Ownership

To maintain power and ownership of Black slaves, the Europeans dehumanized them, as seen from the sample-story of Marie-Joseph. There are more gruesome examples to select on the topic of Black slaves and punishments received in the colonial eras.

It is without reservation that I ponder on the similarities between the aggressive methods of punishment of Black slaves and the systematically more subtle manner in which punishment is disproportionately meted out to Black boys in today's seemingly modern day.

It is chillingly déjà vu.

CHAPTER TWO
THE EVIDENCE OF BLACK STEREOTYPES

A review of history and the perception of Europeans towards Blacks would provide some context to the lingering perception that subtly or non-subtly remains in our modern society about Blacks living in the Western world.

In her publication, the author, Benn-John, acknowledges that Europeans gave meaning to the Black complexion by inferring that *"Blackness connoted invisibility, inferiority and being marked dirty."* This would imply the beginning of a mindset that considered a Black person to be 'chattel' or 'property' for the European colonists to sell, manage, or handle as deemed fit.

With this mindset, the colonists developed a racial hierarchy system where Black people were considered inferior to Whites.

History's Views on How to Govern a Black Person

In her works cited, Benn-John referred to a note by the writer Goldberg. The note revealed that colonizers maintained governance by positioning Blacks as a "worthless, evil, and backward 'Other.'"

The ability to view Blacks as "Other" recommends a European psychological distancing from the possibility that "Other" was a human being. Therefore, in this context, it is not surprising that there are records of brutal exploitation of Black bodies where the Europeans exhibited violence on the Black slaves, raped the women, and, in some cases, forced the enslaved men to produce future labourers in a most primitive forced breeding manner. This seemed possible as long as "Other" was not being considered as a human who had a right to life, dignity, and a reasonable degree of respect as a person.

The authors Borocz and Sarkar provided viewpoints in their 2012 publication to indicate that there existed a 'White supremacist' mentality among Europeans and such mindset enabled the killing of Blacks without impunity, and the other previously described European attitudes towards them.

The Modern Black and Immigration

More than 50% of Black people were born in Canada, according to a publication in 2011.

This suggests that most Black Canadians are *not* immigrants. While the prejudices that Black immigrants experience is a different study from the current discourse, it does not exclude immigrants from the historical biases experienced by Blacks who are born and bred in Canada.

As a result, for the purposes of this writing, there is no separation between the Black immigrant or the Black Canadian living in Canada.

With respect to their treatment in the school system, the result is the same.

The Colonial Legacy and Positioning of Black Boys

The purpose of this book is to propound a theory.

The theory: *The legacy of colonialism has an implication on how Black boys are positioned by teachers in Ontario's K-12 schools.*

I reference a recent article from the popular magazine *Huffington Post*.

The magazine followed the story of a Black student in an Ontario school who testified about an incident he experienced in the classroom.

The student described that he had worn the hood of his shirt over his head in class. The teacher had reportedly provided the following feedback to him for doing so: *"This is not the basketball court. I know you want to be there right now; maybe you'd understand if I say 'Yo yo yo.'"*

The boy's experience appears to be a classic example of how Black boys are viewed by the school system, per this specific incident from Ontario.

As the Black population was considered as "invisible, inferior, or other," from a historical basis, the microaggression experienced in schools reaffirms this theory. For instance, was this Black student whose story was featured in *Huffington Post* possessing a lesser desire to gain an education, like other students from different races?

Why was he considered to have only an interest in the basketball court during his schooling experience?

The student's teacher made some rather specific comments that were glaringly stereotypical. This raises the question: Could there be a need for neutrality training for educators with regards to how to respond to different students' cultural backgrounds? For instance, a stereotype that Black boys in schools may be more interested in athletic pursuits is probably a view that may need to be removed through culturally responsive training.

Most individuals would readily agree that the maintained positioning and exploitation of Black *bodies* continues in twenty-first-century schools.

A publication sheds insight into this stereotype: Teachers position Black boys as having "athletic" bodily characteristics and talent. It implies a lack of intellectual intelligence amongst Black boys, and seems to indicate that these children are useful or interested only in athletic or 'physically-intense' careers.

For anyone who is able to note the correlation between the stereotype placed upon Black boys and their interests in sports and physical conquests only, compared with the colonial era and physical labour, there seems to be a modern expectation, from a Western perspective, that the Black person prefers physical labour-type work.

The 'physical intensive' career was the same type of employment that was available to Blacks in the colonial era. For this reason, intellectual capacity was not a consideration for Black careers since colonial history.

Given this legacy of colonization that has led to microaggressions and blatant stereotypes of Black boys in modern-day schools, it is through this lens that the discussion on positioning theory and an understanding of positionality will progress.

CHAPTER THREE
POSITIONING THEORY AND AN UNDERSTANDING OF POSITIONALITY

To provide a simple introduction, positioning means using human psychology that is both vague and contains elements of multiplicity to judge a situation or a person.

The authors of this notion argued that the psychological composition of humans contains vagueness and multiplicity. In other words, *human beings view circumstances and each other under different perceptions.* Those human perceptions are not necessarily true, or otherwise, they are 'vague.'

Based on this multiplicity of humans, it follows that the way a person classifies other people or groups is based on perspectives they have gathered that are mixed together from various sources; a multiplicity of views that may not necessarily yield the true picture about the person or group that is being judged.

This would explain how or why different groups may classify the Black race under perspectives that may or may not be true. This classification phenomenon is known as 'positioning.'

Davies and Harre defined positioning, in their publication, as, "the discursive process whereby selves are located in conversations as observably and subjectively coherent participants in jointly produced storylines. *There can be interactive positioning in which what one person says positions another. And there can be reflexive positioning in which one positions oneself.*"

There are two types of positioning: Interactive and reflexive. Based on Davies' and Harre's definition of positioning in their 2012 publication (which was defined in the previous paragraph), it is apparent to see that the type of positioning by which teachers place Black boys is of the interactive kind; It means that what a teacher says about the student will determine how the student is positioned in the school community.

Micro and Macro Positioning

It is important to examine positionality based on how teachers position Black boys.

The studies in the publication by Walton, Moore, and Jones in 2019 emphasize that positionality can operate within a micro-level or macro-level of a social structure.

In a school's social structure, positionality operates within a micro-level.

What does micro-level positioning mean?

It means - Small details. Daily interactions.

A school, as a social unit, is a community where individuals from various other communities would gather. Therefore, in a little community, little details matter.

For instance, in the same magazine publication by *Huffington Post* about the life of an Ontario Black schoolboy, the boy described his experiences at a micro-level, including an incident that occurred on the school's playground. He spoke about an instance when he had been playing a ball game with another boy from another race in the schoolyard. After scoring a goal, the non-Black boy he was playing with accused him of cheating on the game and said to the Black boy, *"Thank God; God didn't make me Black like you."*

The non-Black boy did not face any reprimands from the school with regards to his statements.

One may wonder - What were the small details that the non-Black boy had viewed, out of a multiplicity of perspectives that he may have been exposed to, to come to the conclusion that he should thank the divine for not making him Black? This statement is of concern and remains prevalent in our school culture.

In my professional view, such a statement is of concern.

It would imply that our society does not pay the needed attention to the micro-level details of views that position people into stereotypes. In the context of this book, the school system is a huge pot of micro-level details or interactions that form the basis of the whole student experience.

Let us consider the micro-level positioning of the teacher and the non-Black student that interacted with the Black boy in the previously mentioned *Huffington Post* article.

If a teacher believes that a Black boy is fit especially for basketball and not intellectual pursuits (a teacher's position) and a non-Black student believes that he is fortunate for not being Black (a student's positioning) and the school system did not find any issue with such statements (the school's policy positioning), it would follow that *Black boys in the school system have been positioned based on the micro-level subjective opinions of individuals* who form the community, positioned by the school system, and in fact, positioned by the decision-making body that determines the policies of the school system.

The Social Structure as the Determiner of Positioning

"Social structure is a multidimensional space."

This citation from a *Blau* publication could not be more eloquent.

It reaffirms the sentiments that I had raised in the previous section of this book: The students, the teachers, the school policies are a community of bodies that form a multidimensional space, with each player in the space engaged in a part that determines how the social system is structured.

It means that micro-level views are already pre-judged before people interact with groups such as Black boys in schools.

The micro-level views, also previously discussed, are a function of the multiplicity of human perspectives. They are pre-determined by the personal biases of teachers and other students and they are pre-determined by a school policy system that has not evolved away from the primal status of colonialism.

In other words – There are several biases that have built the current Ontario school system, and therefore influence how Black schoolboys are treated:

Biases built from views that Black people are fit only for physical exertion or labour (since Black boys are so 'athletic') instead of intellectualism or that Black people have historically been the recipient of physical punishments as a way of life in slavery days or that Black is classified as 'inferior and other' is the ruling dominion that judges the life and treatment of Black boys in the school system.

Consequences of Thinking 'Outside' the Social Structure

There are certain identity markers that society has forced upon groups.

For instance, a teacher may typically be expected to be a White male or female. This was the predisposition of society until as recently as the turn of the century. Such an identity marker does not go against the norm or grain of western society as it has existed for a few centuries.

In a similar vein, an identity marker of a Black boy as being only useful in athletics (or in some cases, music) has stereotyped the child as being non-intelligent in other areas. Such a positioning does not go against the grain of western social culture. In fact, it seems to be expected. These are socially acceptable identity markers.

It goes without saying, therefore, that identity markers that place an individual outside these comfortable social beliefs are not often well-received.

It could be the reason why an Ontario school teacher would suggest to a Black boy in the classroom that the boy can only understand basketball, per the *Huffington Post* article earlier narrated in this book.

As a result, identity markers such as these are already pre-determining the decisions made towards Black boys in society. It impacts their experiences. In the case of the Black boy in the Ontario school system, the implications of these identity markers are clearly negative.

If society is viewing Black boys as undesirable (Thank God I am not Black", said the non-Black student to the Black boy) or the teacher is viewing them as unintelligent ("I know you want to be on the basketball field"), then what is the *reflexive* response of such a Black child who is hearing all these stereotypes?

The educated answer: The Black schoolboys would consider themselves less than acceptable, as inferior, as undesirable, and as unintelligent.

The results: The Black boys tend to perform below their potential in school.

The conclusion: The Black boys have been positioned by the educational culture.

This analysis gives meaning to the role that educational culture plays in how teachers position Black boys in Ontario's K-12 schools.

As a society, when will we begin to recognize that our positioning of each other impacts the society as a whole - Especially negatively?

As a society, how can a non-Black person conclude that not being Black excludes them from the collateral damage that Blacks face in the societal stereotypes that Blacks are interactively positioned into?

As a society, how can we conclude that operating under the norms, cultures, and values of a colonial era, an ancient practice, an outdated belief system, would enable us to advance for the *general peace of mind and well-being* of our individual families and communities in modern times?

For these reasons, I developed a conceptual framework of positioning, implications, and culturally responsive teaching (PICRT) that is intended to provide some guidance on how we can become victorious over these negative implications that the current societal positioning has placed upon Black boys in the school system.

We will discuss my framework of positioning, implications, and culturally responsive teaching (PICRT) in Chapter Nine of this book.

CHAPTER FOUR

INTERACTIVE POSITIONING OF BLACK BOYS BY TEACHERS

Education in Ontario is a service that should be accessible to everyone without prejudice and regardless of their disabilities, race, origin, religion, sexual orientation, or socio-economic background. The Ontario Human Rights Commission (2018) in a report, indicates:

The scope of "educational services" will include the mastery of knowledge, academic standards, evaluation and accreditation. It may also encompass the development of a student's personality, talents, and mental and physical abilities to their fullest potential, and may include co-instructional activities such as school-related sports, arts and cultural activities, and school functions and field trips (p. 16).

In the previous chapters, I spoke about my views, supported by theories and studies of authors, about the Ontario educational culture.

It is stereotypically biased toward Black boys.

It adopts an ancient colonial practice of labels about the treatment of Black students.

It allows teachers to reflexively determine the positioning of a Black boy based on preconceived biases or school policies that may profess to adopt equality but do not implement it.

Therefore, according to the Ontario Human Rights Commission, if education includes the "mastery of knowledge, academic standards, evaluation and accreditation," the role that the current educational culture plays in positioning is not only a *violation* of the code, but also creates a deficit in educational activities for Black boys.

Teachers are Deficient in Cultural Awareness

As a result of their interactions with students, teachers have the inherent ability to position a child in a certain classification that may or may not be positive.

As mentioned in previous sections of this book, this is known as interactive positioning.

It sheds light on deficiencies in the cultural awareness of teachers.

The teacher as the institutional actor who has a role to play in positioning the Black boy in the educational system may be in need of an education with regards to how their biases, comments, and in fact, micro-level interactions with the student could impact the overall experience and position of the child.

Allies of Black boys agree with the author, Allen, in his 2017 publication, where it is asserted that teachers are institutional actors due to the role they play in positioning these boys.

In addition, Allen contends that these teachers are predominantly White, middle-class, and female.

Furthermore, although teachers are required to work within the scope of the educational services, the testimonials of interpersonal interactions that occur between teachers and Black boys in the Ontario school system suggests that educators place Black children in a compromised position because the legacy of colonialism suggests that Black is the 'other' (Not a fully integrated member of society) is deeply embedded in the way most people see these Black students.

This plays out in the social construct of the educational institution.

Several works cited validate each other, namely Allen (2017) citing Coopersmith (2009), Ladson-Billings (2006), Milner (2013), and Warren (2015), to state that teachers "regularly draw upon *dominant pathologizing discourses* when thinking about, interacting with, and talking about their black male students."

In other words, the treatment and judgment allotted to the Black student are predisposed, as a result of dominant conversations that recommend racial inequality.

"Dominant Pathologizing Discourses"

What are these *dominant pathologizing discourses* that take place amongst educators, per the studies of these scholars?

Here is the meaning: Teachers or school communities consider Black boys as follows - *The masculinity of the Black male is deviant, culturally deficient, not disciplined, hypermasculine, hyperphysical, hypersexual, disruptive, troublemakers, at-risk, and insubordinate which often results in their surveillance and disciplines.*

These stereotypes have been confirmed by testimonials of Black boys in the school system.

In their narratives, these Black students describe their experiences as a consequence of being misunderstood; that teachers use racial stereotypes of their masculinities to contextualize their behaviours.

As such, one of the students cited in Allen's publication (named Andre) indicated that his behaviours are positioned as defiant or anti-intellectual.

Another student (Dontay) indicated that his teachers position Black boys as bad or gangster.

Consequently, and according to Dontay, teachers look at these boys differently than other racial groups, and observe them as troublemakers because the stereotype about them recommends hypermasculinity or violence to be their personalities.

Taken together, the legacy of colonialism is parallel to the actual experiences of Black boys in modern school systems. Whereas colonialism policed Blacks as inferior, and as slave labour with punishment for infractions as seen in an earlier story of a Canadian slave described in this book; the modern system polices Black boys as a legacy of that era of inferior members of society who are liable for punishment of infractions because they are not considered as members of the larger, superior society.

Racism Towards Immigrants

Racialization of Black boys means defining them as immigrants as a whole.

As mentioned earlier, Black people first arrived in Canada in the 1600s, and today, 50% are Canadian born.

In addition, a Toronto District School Board (TDSB) census portrait indicates that most Black students (77%) were born in Canada.

A research study suggests that teachers' stratification of Black boys as immigrants erases their history, contributing to their feeling out of place in schools.

Further, it indicates that "Black students are less likely to feel that staff respect their background, or that school rules fairly apply to them."

The overall result is that Canada's attempt to maintain an image as an egalitarian, multicultural state is a failure.

It erases Black people, symbolically and materially, from their place in Canada's histories and landscapes.

It classifies Blacks as foreigners, fresh arrivals, and recent immigrants to Canada.

It places the Black student at risk when classified by a society based on labels.

CHAPTER FIVE
THE BLACK BOY AT RISK

In addition to race stratification, further studies demonstrate that Black boys are "at-risk" of being deprived of a place in society because the stereotypes about them connotes fatherless, athletes, troublemakers, and underachievers, causing a deficit in their educational activities.

What does this mean?

There can be no confidence for Black boys in gaining an education through a system that believes they are better suited for alternate pursuits that are outside the classroom or at the worst, does not belong in that institution because of a propensity for antisocial behaviour, which sums up the views held toward Black males in general.

These identifications disenfranchise Black boys, and it is no wonder they feel out of place in school and do poorly academically.

Consider the story of Charline Grant.

In an online publication by "The Star", Grant alluded to racial incidents on more than one occasion, involving her eldest son in the Ontario school system.

With these repeated incidents of racially induced events, as alleged by Grant, perhaps it is no wonder that a Black student may feel out of place in the school system when more attention is being paid to the colour of his skin, and the stereotypes of a colonial era, rather than the capacities of his intellect.

Black Boys Are Known As "Athletic"

In a similar vein, in Canadian K-12 schools, teachers give Black boys an athletic stratification with basketball named as the preferred sport.

In his publication, the author, James, sheds light on how teachers position

Black boys as having "athletic" bodily characteristics and talent.

As well, in another book, it is mentioned that teachers and coaches in Toronto who have engaged in the stereotype of Black boys having "natural" athletic abilities have created and maintained construction of them as "naturals" or doing "what they do best" – Sports and athletic pursuits.

This stratification results in more harm than good.

How?

It creates the space for Black boys to "accept" their athleticism as a gift that allows for their underachievement in educational activities. Therefore, with this stratification and the identification of not being smart intellectually, they are often encouraged to play on sports teams rather than focusing on academic pursuits.

The story of Sam, published in a focus group study, attests to this experience.

In the Greater Toronto Area, a student named Sam stated that his teacher tried to get him into sports instead of helping him with math.

It would appear the teacher may have believed that he should consider athletic pursuits as opposed to intellectual goals.

Is It Only Sports?

I don't contend that many Black boys have athletic prowess.

However, does it mean that they are only athletically inclined with no other talents?

Statistically speaking, it is impossible for an entire race of boys to be intelligent in only one thing: Sports.

Science seems to have proven that humans, including Blacks, have a diversity of genetic capabilities that drives the levels of their intelligence.

Although some Black boys possess natural athletic abilities, it does not follow that their being athletic connotates that they are good at nothing else.

"Abilities Segregation"

There is a racial stratification, and it is debilitating to the actual abilities and potential achievements that such Black boys could attain, but for the fact that he is segregated into a box of "athletes only."

I coin a term for this. It should be known as Ability Segregation: Putting a person in a particular box to indicate that he can only perform the abilities available in that box. For instance, basketball.

Consequences of Ability Segregation

One of the consequences of being segregated into one particular type of achievement potential, to the exclusion of all others, is the neglect of schoolwork.

A focus on athletic ability alone takes away the educational and intellectual capacities of the Black boy.

It becomes prejudicial.

The ideal scenario should be a support system that strengthens the students' talents, especially intellectually, while encouraging their physical capabilities, *if they so desire to pursue that area or to develop it.*

A Focus Group of Athletes

James (2019) conducted a focus group in 2018 with nine Black boys in the GTA, aged 12 – 14, all of whom played on the school's sports team.

The boys shared their experiences in school and indicated that their teachers and peers (primarily White) "had perceptions of them as athletes, disrupters, troublemakers, lawbreakers ..."

The boys also indicated their teachers thought negatively of them and provided specific examples of the following:

- Marc noted that a student (Tre) informed him that their teachers engaged in racial stereotypes, locating all Black boys as basketball players.

- Jaden recounted a time he was reprimanded because another student was talking to him in class. Jaden believed the reason he got into trouble when he was paying attention to the teacher was that he is Black.

- Jay noted that his friend informed him that one day he and a group of friends were greeting each other when a teacher came up to them and asked if they were drug dealers. His friend mentioned that he felt badly by the teacher's remark.

- Anderson concurred with Jay's friend's experience, sharing a similar experience. He relayed that if there is a group of coloured kids, teachers automatically think that they are a group of troublemakers.

In these narratives, the participants shared their experiences, thus adding depth to the claim of how teachers in Ontario's K-12 schools position Black boys.

CHAPTER SIX
IMPLICATIONS OF POSITIONING

Teachers' positioning of Black boys brings about some implications.

Research shows that the implications of positioning include:

- increased surveillance

- streaming

- detentions

- suspensions

- expulsions

In addition, findings suggest that Black boys who are positioned will either adapt or resist the positioning being given to them.

I want to focus on the specific effects of streaming on Black boys.

Effects of Positioning

The effect of Black boys' positioning by teachers results in the neoliberal practices of streaming. Wotherspoon (2004) defines streaming as a *"formal and informal educational mechanisms that sorts students based on ability, social background, or other characteristics into groups, programs, or institutions that have differential status."*

The Story of Ms. Benn-John

Benn-John was prime and ready to go to university.

She made an appointment with her guidance counsellor to discuss her higher education options.

Instead, she received unexpected counselling from the educator: That she did not have what it took to go for higher education.

This is a classic example of *streaming.* When an authority figure attempts to 'stream' a student towards a particular result, whether or not it is the best decision for the student.

Benn-John proved the educator wrong.

She went to university and moved up to the point where she was now ready to begin Ph.D. level studies.

A Story by the Author - My 18-Year-Old

My 18-year-old son was told by a Toronto District School Board teacher to take applied courses because obtaining a trade is also rewarding.

The teacher was right in that tradesmanship is a rewarding profession.

However, when a student expresses his or her interest in going to university, it should be supported.

It would seem that the trades were the implied fitting vocation for my 18-year-old, as opposed to other options that may include 4-year university studies.

This was classic streaming.

A Story by the Author - My 20-Year-Old

My 20-year-old expressed his desire to go to university to pursue industrial design.

His York Region District School Board teacher told him to consider college and recommended one "that has a good program."

Now, I ask: Why would the educator profile my son for a 2-year college as opposed to a 4-year course of study?

I mentioned the effects of reflexive interactions earlier in this book – How a person's subjective views can be impacted by the way society judges them.

My reflexive position as an educator enabled me to recognize that my sons were being streamed by their teachers.

Today, my 20- and 18-year-olds are university students.

Yet – Before this successful story, they were *streamed.*

They chose the path that was right and true for them, and not the opinions of educators who tried to stream them, who believed they belonged to a particular academic box.

CHAPTER SEVEN
STREAMING AND THE BLACK STUDENT EXPERIENCE

James' 2018 focus group findings acknowledge that Black students in the GTA, particularly males, tend to be streamed into non-academic programs and that teachers tend to observe them – unfortunately, in negative lights - in and out of the classroom.

Apart from academic 'sorting,' one of the features of streaming, this book has continuously mentioned the unequal punishments that students are given in schools based on their races.

It is another representation of streaming.

The example statements of the Black boys from the studies revealed that teachers performed "surveillance of them (for purposes of punishing misbehaviour) while other students who exhibited similar or worse behaviour went unpunished or received lighter punishment."

The Data Paints the Picture

Between school years 2011-16, TDSB issued 307 expulsions, 94% were secondary school students with the majority (89%) being male.

A point that needs emphasizing is that Black students account for almost half (48%) of those expulsions.

One may think that the number of Black students facing punishment, in comparison to other students, is high because there are more Black students represented in the Ontario school system. Right?

After all, logistically speaking, if the population of a certain sample is higher, the probability of it being selected for events is higher.

Unfortunately, this is not the case with the current data. Statistics reveal that Black students accounted for 36.2% of the TDSB population from 2016 to 2017 and they were 34.3% from 2017 to 2018.

As they represent less than half of the school population, why are they experiencing *almost half* of the school expulsions?

This concludes that Black boys are highly overrepresented in detentions, suspensions, and expulsions.

Children Adapting to Positioning and Repositioning

So far, I have provided definitions of positioning and streaming.

Positioning means *using human psychology that is both vague and contains elements of multiplicity, to judge a situation or a person.*

Streaming means *formal and informal educational mechanisms that sorts students based on ability, social background, or other characteristics into groups, programs, or institutions that have differential status."*

An educator in a school system can position a student, based on the educator's vague and various perspectives (which may or may not be true) about the student's ethnicity or background. Such position can be the determinant of whether a student receives the quality of education that makes them grow in their intellectual capacities or if, instead, they would be denied such development.

The educator has the ability to position a student in such a manner through reflexive interaction – Judging the child based on the teacher's perspectives of who the group or race to which the child belongs.

When this happens, and a Black child, for instance, finds himself positioned by his teacher as 'good for basketball' but not for intellectual pursuits, the child would invariably adapt to the opinion of such a person of authority – Their educator.

This means that, potentially, Black students would adapt or reposition themselves based on these positioning events.

In my experience as a mother, I have observed where teachers position Black boys in Ontario K-12 schools.

As a York Region parent of two Canadian-born Black boys who underwent these stratifications, I remember confronting these issues with teachers. When they realized that I was an educator and married, they dimed their classification regarding my sons. I then realized the powerful role intersectionality plays in the lives of Black boys.

All the same, my boys repositioned themselves mainly because they recognized that they were being streamed into an identity that contradicts who they are and knowing the value we place on education by telling them it is primarily how they will succeed in the Canadian Eurocentric system.

Effects of Black Boys Adapting to Positioning

Adaptation based on the reflexive positioning of society is damaging to Black boys' educational success when they enroll in non-university programs due to recommendation by a teacher.

Moreover, punishments meted out with the measures based on the students' racial background are disruptive of their intellectual progress.

The punishments received for infractions trigger down to missed instruction time, class activities, in-class work, and assessments.

Research suggests that this causes a deficit in educational success, resulting in high dropout rates.

Let us consider the data.

Follert's 2021 research publication indicates where "new data from the Durham District School Board (DDSB) shows Black students are faring worse academically than their white and South Asian classmates." In addition, the new data also reveals where Black students had higher proportions of suspensions compared to their counterparts. This recent data shows an educational quandary for Black students in Ontario's K-12 schools.

The dropout rate of Black students in Canada is over 40%.

When the drop-out rate data is disaggregated by gender, *the percentage is much higher for Black male students.*

It was further confirmed that Toronto, which is the largest city in Canada, has the highest dropout rate of Black students and that they are "over-represented in vocational schools and underrepresented in advanced level programs in relation to the rest of the school populations."

One may wonder as to the reason for this pattern of underrepresentation of Black boys in universities.

After all, if the evidence of studies provided in this book so far recommends that Black boys are positioned for marginal intellectual pursuits, then it follows that the reality, as presented by the data I mentioned above, confirms the views that have been laid out so far.

In a similar example, further findings indicate that Black students in Toronto, particularly males, perform poorly academically and lack the qualifications to apply to post-secondary institutions. When they are qualified to enter post-secondary, they are least likely to go to university, with 50% of them entering a graduate program.

Self Fulfilling Prophecy

It has been suggested that while some Black boys possess innate athletic abilities, the identification of Black boys being "natural" athletes can enable them to adapt to this positioning by over-dedicating their time to playing sports while taking time away from other social roles and educational activities.

Research has shown that where some Toronto teachers and coaches in good faith supported, nurtured, and developed Black boys' athletic interest, the identification of "natural" athletic talent causes these boys to own this position by fulfilling their natural potential and making this a viable substitute for their educational success.

CHAPTER EIGHT
ZERO TOLERANCE

"Zero Tolerance" is a term that emerged in relation to drug enforcement.

In the 1990s, Ontario decided to adopt the term – For a different reason.

In Ontario, zero tolerance was intended to represent policies and procedures that punish misbehaviours in the school system and to create a safe learning environment

Unfortunately, the application of 'zero tolerance' appears to be disproportionate as it relates to race.

Data suggests that the implementation of the zero tolerance policies have attributed to the contribution of racial stereotypes and marginalization through the manifestation of positioning by school personnel.

To put it succinctly – The Black child is punished more.

Considering it from Canada's point of view, zero tolerance was necessary to maintain the safety of stakeholders in schools. After all, there has always been a history of disciplinary policies and procedures for unacceptable behaviours in Ontario schools through corporal punishments, as represented by policies such as the 1993 *Safe Schools Policy on Violence and Weapons* by the Scarborough Board of Education (the first zero-tolerance approach in Ontario), the April 2000 zero tolerance policy across Ontario schools, the September 2001 *Code of Conduct*, and the *Safe Schools Act*.

Zero Tolerance and Minority Students

Over the past years, there has been much contention regarding the controversial application of zero tolerance policies and procedures to minority students, which led to several inquiries and actions by the Ontario Human Rights Commission (OHRC).

It was noted that in the Greater Toronto Area (GTA), and other parts of Ontario, the Safe Schools Act and school board policies are having a disproportionate impact on racial minority students, particularly Black students, and students with disabilities.

Due to these unfavourable public denouncements, the Ontario Ministry of Education took steps to eradicate zero tolerance from ministry documents. After all, in a CBC News interview, it was revealed that an agreement was reached to amend the Province's Safe Schools Act and the removal of the words "zero tolerance" from all ministry documents.

Changes Made – But Was There Really Change?

Although these changes were made, and zero tolerance was stricken off policy documents, there has been no change to the minority student environment.

The dropout rate remains slightly steady, and there is a continued high suspension and expulsion rate among minority students with Black students mostly impacted.

The reality, therefore, demonstrates that though 'zero tolerance' no longer exists in policy, its application is ingrained in the positioning that teachers or educators place upon Black students.

The conclusion is that removing zero tolerance from school policy is not a substitute for culturally responsive teaching.

Why Do We Need Culturally Responsive Teaching?

The Ontario Ministry of Education mandated Ontario school boards to develop an action plan to support expelled students with the continuity of their education.

Unfortunately, data confirms that these plans do not support students.

Between the school years 2011 - 2016, an astounding 58% of the expelled students in Toronto who participated in the program "dropped out of school or did not have a known destination."

The effectiveness of a program depends on the people who are running it.

If there is a program for supporting expelled students, and the program fails, what could be the reason?

Funding?

Funding is an unlikely excuse as long as the program is *being supported by the government.*

Therefore, if the program is funded, what hinders it from success but the commitment or ability of those who implement it?

This lack of change suggests a need for Culturally Responsive Teaching (CRT) for all Ontario K-12 schoolteachers.

CHAPTER NINE
AN ADOPTION OF CULTURALLY RESPONSIVE TEACHING (CRT)

The issue of Black boys' positioning necessitates the adoption of Culturally Responsive Teaching.

This brings us to the framework that I alluded to in Chapter 2.

The culturally responsive teaching system requires some approaches to make it successful. Let us consider the approaches now.

How to Have Successful Culturally Responsive Teaching

1. Educators may find it difficult to accept that the schooling system is hardwired to maintain the racial inequities into which children are born. The first step to removing the hardwiring can only be achieved through teachers' decolonization of self.

In view of that, how can Ontario K-12 teachers decolonize themselves?

a. **Decolonize and Personalize Learning:** Decolonizing teachers requires that educators examine their cultural biases, and learn about marginalized people's culture which includes reading about their culture and history, talking with community leaders or elders, and inviting them to the classrooms as guest speakers, attending cultural events, adding cultural books to the class library, incorporating the individual cultures represented in the classroom to the lessons, and by meditating to confront biases. Consequently, from a continuum lens, the decolonization of self leads to adopting a culturally responsive teaching practice.

b. **Familiarize with Students Culture:** Teachers need to make CRT the fabric of their practice, which means teachers must take the necessary steps and, by all means possible, learn about the different cultures represented in their classroom, and incorporating the cultures in the class experiences.

c. **Include Teachers Preparatory Programs:** In eradicating the issue of positioning, CRT must not only be adopted by practicing teachers but must also be implemented in the teacher preparation programs i.e., pre-service teachers.

d. **Teachers Do Not Need to Be Cultural Experts**: While these suggestions recommend a learning program for teachers that will acclimate them to other cultures, this does not mean that the teacher needs to be an expert on all cultural competencies. To learn, teachers should take advantage of the cultural resources in their community.

e. **Include Relevant Material in Class Packages**: In addition, teachers can include in their practice "culturally relevant educational materials and a schooling environment that captures their imagination and interest in academic work." This would make them competent to work within the scope of the Ontario educational services, which would inform Black boys' educational success.

Feedback from Black Students About CRT

Evidence suggests that Black students experience when learning about diversity is 'tick the box.'

In other words, their experience with cultural learning in schools is meaningless.

For the most part, per their feedback, *"their school, curriculum, and other educational materials were not culturally relevant or responsive to their learning needs, interests, and expectations."*

In fact, one student opined that the only time their culture is reflected in their learning experience is during February's Black History Month celebration. This brings to the forefront the need for curriculum developers to integrate Black history into the curriculum.

Apparently, the voice of the Black student has not been heard with regards to areas of interest that they would like to have included in their learning experience.

A Toronto District School Board census found that "most Black students say that learning more about their own culture or race would make learning more interesting for them (78%), help them enjoy school more (66%), and help them do better in school (56%)."

The data supports the argument for teacher's immersion in a CRT program.

Culturally responsive teaching should be a core component of the K12 teachers' training curriculum.

Conceptual Framework

In analyzing research articles, I established a conceptual framework of positioning, implications, and culturally responsive teaching (PICRT) to show the sequential process of the following:

1. **Positioning** - The role educational culture plays in how teachers position Black boys

2. **Implications** - How identification impacts Black boys' education

3. **Culturally Responsive Teaching** - Calls on Ontario K-12 teachers to become an agent of change by adopting a culturally responsive teaching practice to cater to Black boys' educational needs in the classroom. A visualization of this framework (PICRT) is presented in Figure 1.

Figure 1

Illustration of the Sequential PICRT Process Structure

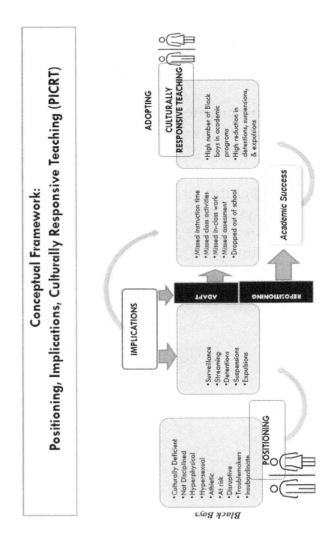

Limitations

It should be recognized that much of the statistical data referred to in this book is confined to the TDSB, which houses the highest population of Black students in Ontario. Additionally, James' (2019) stories of the experiences of Black students was small in size, and thus cannot be overlooked.

Finally, drop-out rates have been criticized for failing to recognize students who re-register in other educational institutions, and it is unlikely that all non-Black teachers position Black boys in pejorative terms, and not all Black male students are streamed in a particular way.

Still, school boards have a legal and moral imperative to ensure that all students are given an equal opportunity to succeed, and research suggests that a recognition of positionality, and the inclusion of CRT.

CHAPTER TEN
CONCLUSION

This research book presented how the legacy of colonialism has affected the educational culture. A history of slavery wherein Black individuals are treated with greater or more extreme punitive measures was discussed.

There was a story about a slave in Quebec, Canada, Marie-Joseph Angélique, who was hung for allegedly setting fire to her master's property.

As well, a comparison of the 'physical' nature of labour performed by Blacks in colonial times, and the expectation that such exertions are the main talent area of Blacks in current times was discussed, as an example, the highly physical careers of sports.

The experience of Black boys and students is not far removed from the historical sentiments. The Black students receive more punishment in comparison to other racial counterparts. This book considered how teachers in Ontario's K-12 schools position Black boys extremely similarly to these archaic sentiments of coloniality, and its implications on the students' educational activities.

This argument above was based on the notion of positioning theory and an understanding of positionality – That the experiences of Black students in the school system are dependent on how their educators view them: If viewed as talented only in sports, their educators or teachers appear to hold no interest in mentoring them into intellectual or academic career areas.

This book also reviewed a conceptual framework of positioning, its implications, and some thoughts in culturally responsive teaching.

As a result of such positioning, Black boys respond by either adapting or repositioning themselves to the way their community, or teachers, view them.

Further, a discussion on Ontario's 'zero tolerance' was raised. The policy had been eliminated; however, its practice remains in the experience of Black boys, and the degree of punishments they receive, in comparison to their other racial counterparts.

This book also presented the adoption of culturally responsive teaching, calling on the first step by teachers to decolonize themselves and, thereafter, inviting teachers to take all the necessary steps to incorporate students' culture in the classroom.

This study demonstrates that teachers use identity markers to position Black boys in Ontario's K-12 schools. They are positioned as immigrants, fatherless, deviant, culturally deficient, not disciplined, hypermasculine, hyperphysical, hypersexual, disruptive, troublemakers, athletic, at-risk, and insubordinate.

Consider the young boy previously mentioned in this book in one of the story examples. His teacher considered him to be inattentive in class because his interests could only be sports or basketball, per the expressed views of the teacher.

These identification markers have negative implications and serve as a deficit to the educational success of these children. Black boys are often streamed into non-academic and trade programs, surveilled, and receive punishment through the application of the maintained zero tolerance for punitive infractions. Time spent out of class results in them falling behind in their educational activities. Hence, Black boys have the highest dropout rate in Canadian schools.

We expect that teachers will fulfill their role to help develop students' personalities, talents, and mental and physical abilities to their fullest potential through culturally responsive teaching practice. We also expect that schools and other institutions would play their role in changing neoliberal policies and procedures and ensure that the changes work in the best interest of all students.

REFERENCES

Allen, Q. (2017). "They write me off and don't give me a chance to learn anything": Positioning, discipline, and Black masculinities in school. *Anthropology & Education Quarterly.* 48. 269-283.

American Psychological Association. (2008). Are zero tolerance policies effective in the schools? An evidentiary review and recommendations. *American Psychological Association. 63*(9). 852-862. https://www.apa.org/pubs/info/reports/zero-tolerance.pdf.

Bailey, J. (2017). From "zero tolerance" to "safe and accepting": Surveillance & equality in the evolution of Ontario's education & policy. *Education Law Journal, 26*(2):*147-180.*

Benn-John, J. (2019). Canada's legacy of colonialism: Implications in education. In F.J.

Villegas & J. Brady (Eds.), *Critical schooling: Transformative theory and practice.* (pp. 75-97). Cham, Switzerland: Palgrave-MacMillan.

Böröcz, J., & Sarkar, M. (2012). Colonialism. In *encyclopedia of global studies*, 1, 229-233. Thousand Oaks, CA: SAGE Publications, Inc.

CBC News. (2007). Ontario agrees to end zero-tolerance school policy. *CBC/Radio-Canada.* https://www.cbc.ca/news/canada/toronto/ontario-agrees-to-end-zero-tolerance-school-policy-1.671464.

Davies, B., & Harré, R. (2007). Positioning: The discursive production of selves. *Journal for the Theory of Social Behaviour.* 20. 43 - 63. https://www.researchgate.net/publication/227980244_Positioning_The_Discursive_Produ   ction_of_Selves

de France, R.C., & Waldron, W.S. (2018). Not 'just' but just: A conversation on diversity, social justice, and culturally responsive teaching. In *educators on diversity, social justice & schooling.* (pp. 77 - 98). Toronto, ON: Canadian Scholars, and imprint of CSP Books Inc.

Dean, A.V. (2018). The gospel of diversity: Performing diversity to create the appearance of institutional change. In *educators on diversity, social justice & schooling.* (pp. 99-117). Toronto,

ON: Canadian Scholars, and imprint of CSP Books Inc.

Follert, J. (2021). Achievement gap: New DDSB data shows Black students faring worse than their classmates. *Durham Region.com.* https://www.durhamregion. com/news-story/10332724- achievement-gap-new-ddsb-data-shows-black-students-faring-worse-than-their- classmates/

Francis, A. (2020). Change is Long Overdue for Black Students in Ontario. These Parents Aren't Waiting on the Government to Make It Happen. www.thestar.com

Gay, G. (2002). Preparing for culturally responsive teaching. *Journal of Teacher Education*, 53, 106-116.

Harris, S. (2020). Black Students Face 'Toxic' Racism Despite Decades of 'Solutions' in Ontario, www.huffingtonpost.ca

Howard, P., & James, C. (2019). When dreams take flight: How teachers imagine and implement an environment that nurtures Blackness at an Africentric school in Toronto, Ontario. *Curriculum Inquiry, 49*(3), 313–337.

https://cmiller.commons.hwdsb. on.ca/2016/10/03/biographies-of-famous-black-canadians/

James, C. (2019). Adapting, disrupting, and resisting: How middle school Black males position themselves in response to racialization in school. *Canadian Journal of Sociology, 44*(4), 373–398.

James, C. E. (2012). Students "at Risk": Stereotypes and the schooling of Black boys. *Urban Education, 47*(2), 464–494.

Josiah Henson (n.d.). https://en.wikipedia.org/wiki/Josiah_Henson

Maynard, R. (2017). The (mis)education of Black youth: Anti-blackness in the school system. In R. Maynard, *Policing Black lives: State violence in Canada from slavery to the present* (pp. 208-228). Halifax: Fernwood.

Miller, C. (n.d.). Biographies of Famous Black Canadians.

Ontario Human Rights Commission. (2018). Policy on accessible education for students with disabilities. *Government of Ontario*. http://www.ohrc.on.ca/en/policy-accessible-education-students-disabilities.

Saul, R. (2006, Winter). How black male student athletes get stereotyped in Canadian schools. *Our Schools, our Selves, 15*, 91-95,97-109.

Thompson, S. (2007). Breaking the links between race, poverty, and achievement. Strategies for school system leaders on district-level change. *Panasonic Foundation, 13*(1), 1-2. https://www. ncsl.org/print/cyf/strategiesforschooleaders.pdf

Toronto District School Board. (n.d.). Trend data fact sheet no. 1. Toronto: Ontario. Toronto District School Board. https://www.tdsb.on.ca/Portals/0/ Community/Community%20Advisory%20 committees/I CAC/research/September%20 2012%20Cohort%20dataAcrobat%20Document. pdf.

Walton, R., Moore, K., & Jones, N. (2019). Positionality. In *technical communication after the social justice turn: Building coalitions for action.* (1st ed., pp. 63–82).

Wotherspoon, T. (2004). The process of schooling. In T. Wotherspoon (2nd ed.), *the sociology of education in Canada: Critical perspectives.* (pp. 91-124). Don Mills, Ontario: Oxford University Press Canada.

Yau, M., O'Reilly, J., Rosolen, L., & Archer, B. (2011). *Census portraits: Understanding our student's ethno-cultural background.* Toronto: Ontario. Toronto District School Board.

Zheng, S. (2019). *Caring and safe schools report 2017 – 2018.* Toronto: Ontario. Toronto District School Board.

Zheng, S., & De Jesus, S. (2017). *Expulsion decision-making process and expelled students' transition experience in the Toronto District School Board's caring and safe schools programs and their graduation outcomes.* (Research Report No. 16/17-15) Toronto: Ontario. Toronto District School Board.

ABOUT THE AUTHOR

Charmaine Simms-Saunders is a college professor, author, and entrepreneur. A lifelong learner who holds a Master of Education (M.Ed.), Bachelor of Education (B.Ed.), Excellence in Educating Adults Recognition of Achievement, Office Administration-Executive Diploma, and Family Supports Certificate.

She is a Business Management and Office Administration Professor who promotes a safe, respectful, and inclusive learning environment. Charmaine believes that each person has a place in the world and her place is evident in the work that she does in the classroom where she practices her ethos.

Her philosophy is simple: *When given the opportunity, we all have the ability to experience transformative learning.*

The motivation behind the writing of this book is driven by her faith in transformative learning: The classroom experience should not be a mere checkbox against a form to indicate that a student passed through that course. Instead, it should be a bespoke, customized system that is tailored to the needs of every student, and geared towards ensuring their success in whatever career interests they may desire to pursue.

Charmaine's experience as a mother, learner, and educator has influenced the development of this book. She is passionate about fostering academic development and success for every student. As a result, she wishes to share this book with curriculum developers, administrators, teachers in Canadian K-12 schools, child care educators, parents, caregivers, and anyone who works with Black youths.

Made in the USA
Monee, IL
27 February 2021